Our Favorite Animals Activities Book

Coloring, Puzzles, Word Games and More

Eileen Coulson

Activity Book
for Kids

This Book belongs to:

_____

_____

_____

Instructions

Instructions for Puzzle Word Search:

Find and circle all of the words that are hidden in the grid, running in one of eight possible directions horizontally, vertically, or diagonally.

Instructions for Maze:

The object of the game is to find a way from the entrance to the exit.

Coloring Pages, Puzzle Word Search and Maze

Animal Puzzle 1

```
m o i n o o p d i h c p y
d n l a i o o h c o o p i
y i a t n c a b r o p o t
r e p t d o g g y u l o n
i n a e a p i t p t g d m
g i c o l a h b e a g l e
l n k h m o e p t p g e i
h a u h a u h i h c a r g
t c o l t s t p z c t g g
h u g n i r e t u e n n o
n o i t a c i t s e m o d
g e s i n p g y o a p m o
o c l h s r l y n p i o t
```

pet
hole
puppy
mongrel
poodle
dalmatian
domestication
pack
pooch
doggie
chihuahua
corgi
trail
tail
chase
beagle
neutering
canine
doggy
spitz

Animal Puzzle 2

```
s  t  m  e  o  w  l  p  p  t
u  p  t  e  n  i  d  m  u  m
d  r  a  p  o  e  l  n  m  o
e  a  c  n  d  w  t  a  a  u
e  u  d  c  t  r  a  t  n  s
r  g  l  d  b  h  i  r  i  e
b  a  i  l  n  b  e  l  p  k
w  j  w  i  b  g  e  r  a  o
b  t  e  a  i  f  u  r  a  r
t  r  r  t  e  p  t  n  c  u
```

lion
meow
sand
tail
jaguar
pet
tiger
leopard
kitten
felis
rat
rabbit
fur
claw
panther
meow
breed
wildcat
puma
mouse

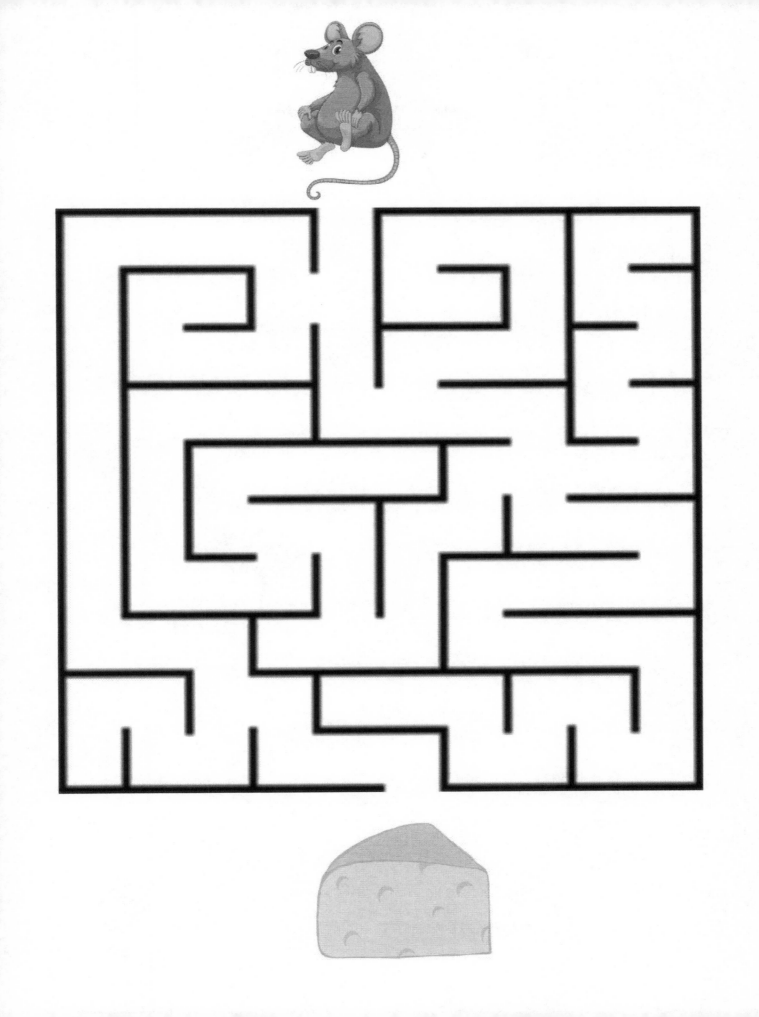

Animal Puzzle 3

```
e i d g b t f e e i z b
s n o o b a b f l o i s
y s n m i a i b o d y l
s e s p r l e l t r m a
t c e w d l o c t e f m
r t l l s g i r e t m m
h s i f y l l e j t n a
s w t m o r g a n i s m
i m p r e d a t o r t m
f e e m l i o u r c e a
t d r i b a a r n m a l
a r w c i n s e c t a r
```

mammal
body
insects
wild
fish
creature
organism
critter
pet
baboon
wildlife
jellyfish
predator
bird
mammals
birds
bone
reptile
insect
zoology

Animal Puzzle 4

```
a m h g g i r a f f e h
r a b b i t l a n e y h
e m d t n l g s z l n y
e m f n i i a n o i l e
d a a r a g a y h d p k
a l o m y p e p n o o n
z g a i m k l r l c s o
r r h i n o c e r o s m
m e h o d d t r t r a o
i c d z m n e h h c r m
l e o p a r d l r o g d
a o e p m b d f o r m o
```

tiger
donkey
chimpanzee
deer
rhinoceros
giraffe
lion
mammoth
mammal
hyena
gorilla
rabbit
crocodile
antelope
monkey
dolphin
panda
grass
leopard
zoo

Animal Puzzle 5

```
m o o s e n p w e i
s e p y r o v i q a
q b r e k s u t g m
u a i r h i n o a l
i b m a a b r a o y
r o a t n f o w l o
r o t a g i l l a e
e n e c o i m t r o
l o o m l w h a l e
t w b e a s t v l a
```

squirrel
frog
cow
alligator
bison
primate
ivory
whale
miocene
angola
moose
beast
pig
tusker
rat
cat
animal
baboon
owl
rhino

Animal Puzzle 6

t	h	r	a	i	b	d	s	r	e	m	r
l	u	z	r	r	e	s	u	r	e	r	r
e	c	d	d	b	e	a	r	g	c	u	m
m	k	r	i	c	s	h	i	p	p	o	t
a	f	a	e	o	o	t	t	e	r	n	g
c	o	z	n	a	t	u	g	n	a	r	o
u	o	i	p	s	t	o	c	o	a	e	b
m	d	l	o	u	l	u	i	a	a	p	m
u	s	y	l	z	z	i	r	g	l	t	u
f	t	l	a	u	u	b	c	e	d	i	j
a	l	n	r	m	e	t	u	r	t	l	e
a	l	a	r	z	c	o	s	d	a	e	e

dinosaur
goat
turtle
snake
reptile
lizard
otter
hippo
camel
creature
orangutan
zebra
panther
jumbo
polar
circus
grizzly
bear
foods
ant

Animal Puzzle 7

```
r a b b i t s r d a p
s p a r r o t d r i b
t s e s a c n m g a a
a c d d a o a s i r o
o o a r c d h t h a o
g s d o i a p y s c r
h n w l r b e r o c a
l s l k f n l o a o g
a o a c a m e r o o n
p e e h s l a m i n a
k o s l l a f g m p k
```

elephants
bird
leaf
sheep
cameroon
hyena
goats
animals
dog
pigs
shark
rabbits
kangaroo
africa
cats
armadillo
parrot
birds
cows
raccoon

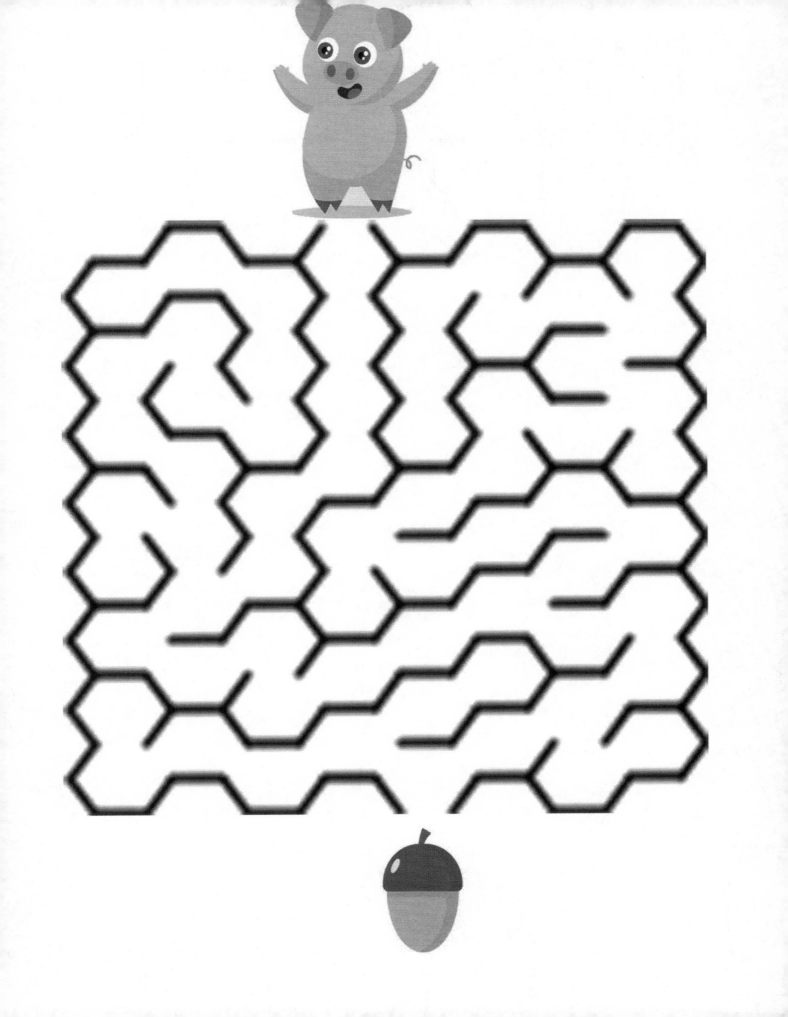

Animal Puzzle 8

```
h a e o n r k a a t n s
o a p i g e o n g p e s
r e e o s t r i c h s e
s t n u h s y e k n o m
e o o l a m b s e b k d
r m g b e a r k t e r o
o u s n i h c u p a c g
b m e g i i r d g s r s
k o k a h t l o s t e t
s l a c l i n r n s g i
m n n e w h a u n i a i
m n s r e t n u h e s k
```

monkeys
dogs
hunting
dragon
hamster
wild
capuchin
mouse
beasts
chickens
hunts
lambs
turtles
horse
snakes
rats
bear
pigeon
ostrich
hunters

Animal Puzzle 9

```
s a o k e m o n k e y s
e m d e s l s c g o l n
l o s s l n n m i t z e
t u h e d g e h o g z s
r s p b f n n k d l i w
u e s e l i d o c o r c
t k t a s h l o g i g n
e a n s o c i d s a h s
g n i t n u h b l o r c
r s r s h p m d r i p d
r e t s m a h s i p w u
e s o t l c e s t e s e
```

crocodiles
wildlife
pet
tree
grizzly
hedgehog
monkeys
dogs
hunting
dragon
hamster
wild
capuchin
mouse
beasts
chickens
lambs
turtles
horse
snakes

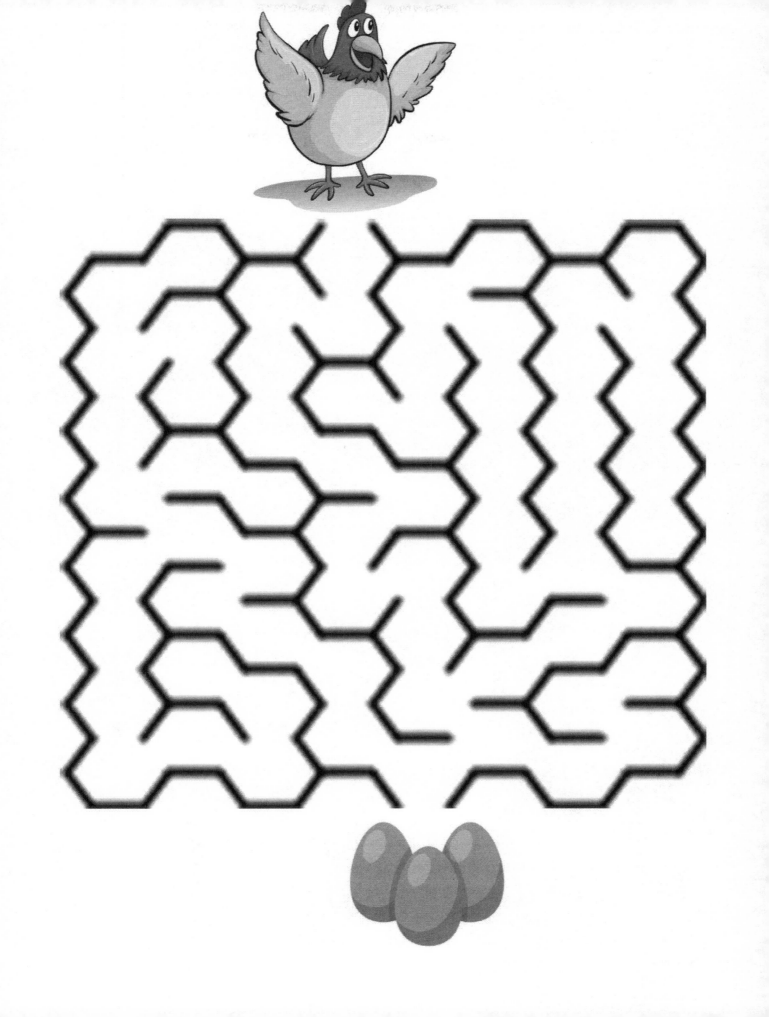

Animal Puzzle 10

```
l a i e g e c k o p e
g j u m p i n g s e c
o n n a m u p g p e h
s r i n m i a p i h a
t t e p o z k n g s s
r n i v e o s l e n e
i h b l a e b e o a s
c h l l c e k a n i t
h e a t a c b o b l a
d e s e r t m a o s r
c a m e l r a e b z e
```

rats
bear
pigeon
ostrich
gazelle
zookeeping
chipmunk
bobcat
koala
snail
beaver
gecko
desert
jumping
baboon
insects
chase
camel
sheep
puma

Solutions for Word Puzzles

and Maze

Animal Puzzle 1

pet
hole
puppy
mongrel
poodle
dalmatian
domestication
pack
pooch
doggie
chihuahua
corgi
trail
tail
chase
beagle
neutering
canine
doggy
spitz

Animal Puzzle 2

lion
meow
sand
tail
jaguar
pet
tiger
leopard
kitten
felis
rat
rabbit
fur
claw
panther
meow
breed
wildcat
puma
mouse

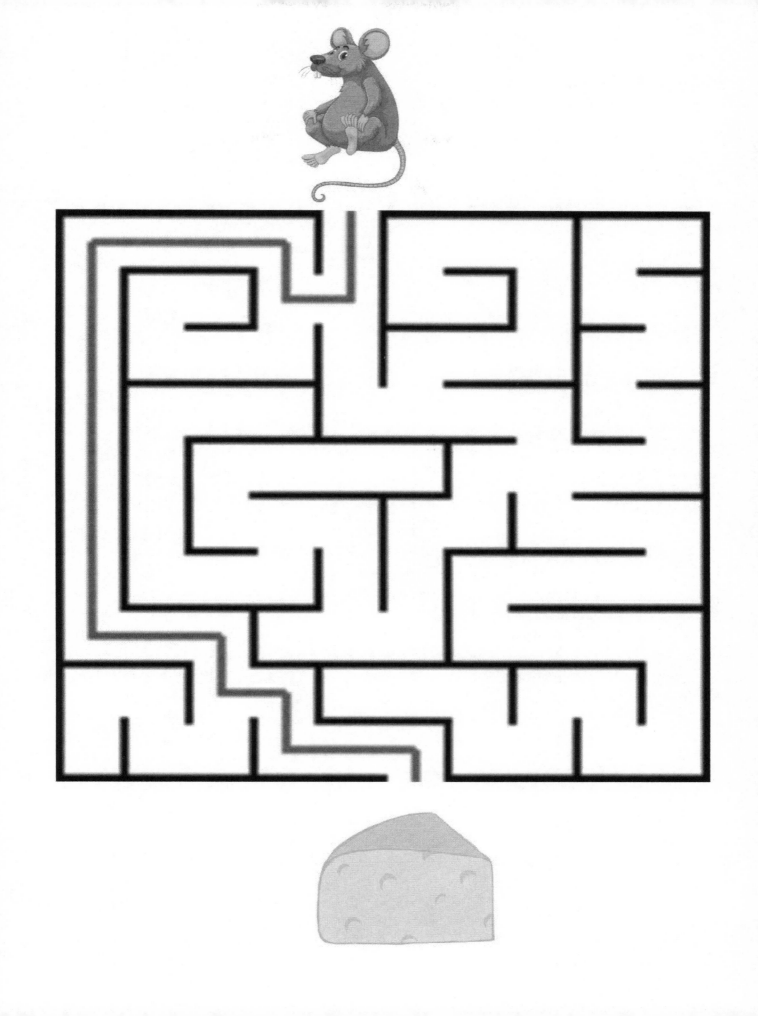

Animal Puzzle 3

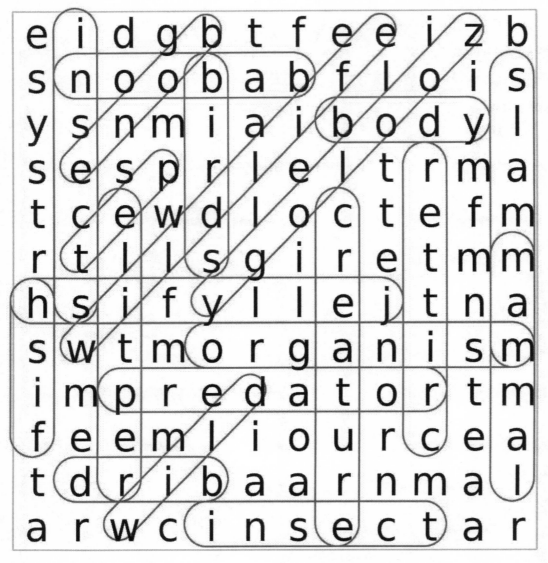

mammal
body
insects
wild
fish
creature
organism
critter
 pet
baboon
wildlife
jellyfish
predator
bird
mammals
birds
bone
reptile
insect
zoology

Animal Puzzle 4

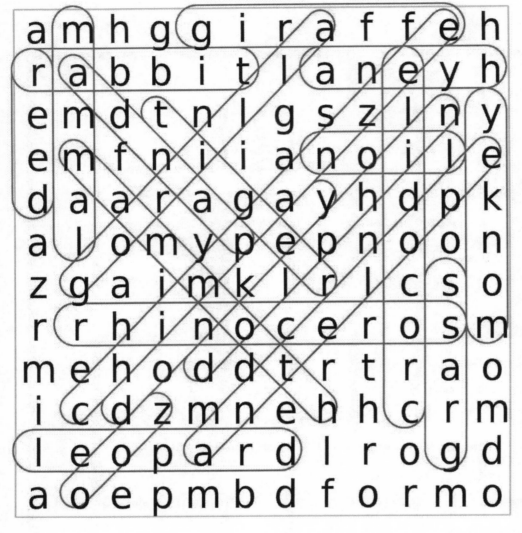

tiger
donkey
chimpanzee
deer
rhinoceros
giraffe
lion
mammoth
mammal
hyena
gorilla
rabbit
crocodile
antelope
monkey
dolphin
panda
grass
leopard
zoo

Animal Puzzle 5

squirrel
frog
cow
alligator
bison
primate
ivory
whale
miocene
angola
moose
beast
pig
tusker
rat
cat
animal
baboon
owl
rhino

Animal Puzzle 6

dinosaur
goat
turtle
snake
reptile
lizard
otter
hippo
camel
creature
orangutan
zebra
panther
jumbo
polar
circus
grizzly
bear
foods
ant

Animal Puzzle 7

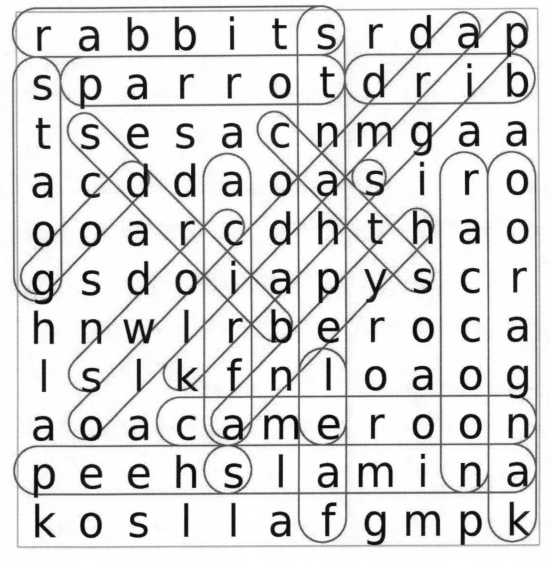

r a b b i t s r d a p
s p a r r o t d r i b
t s e s a c n m g a a
a c d d a o a s i r o
o o a r c d h t h a o
g s d o i a p y s c r
h n w l r b e r o c a
l s l k f n l o a o g
a o a c a m e r o o n
p e e h s l a m i n a
k o s l l a f g m p k

elephants
bird
leaf
sheep
cameroon
hyena
goats
animals
dog
pigs
shark
rabbits
kangaroo
africa
cats
armadillo
parrot
birds
cows
raccoon

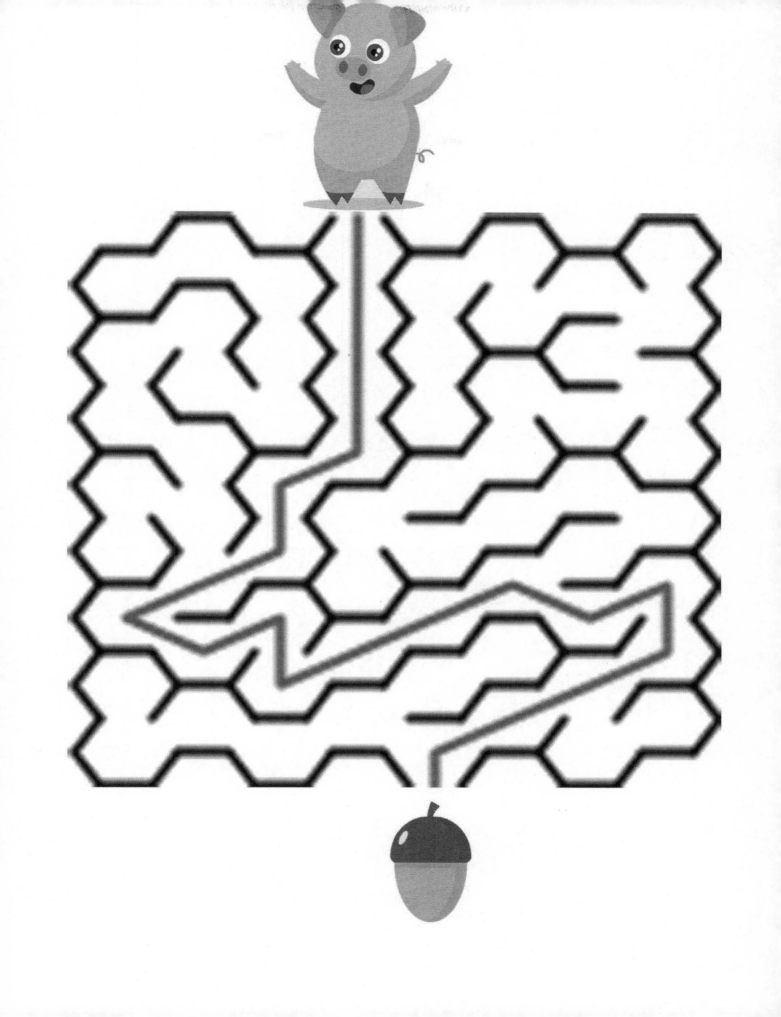

Animal Puzzle 8

```
h a e o n r k a a t n s
o a p i g e o n g p e s
r e e o s t r i c h s e
s t n u h s y e k n o m
e o o l a m b s e b k d
r m g b e a r k t e r o
o u s n i h c u p a c g
b m e g i i r d g s r s
k o k a h t l o s t e t
s l a c l i n r n s g i
m n n e w h a u n i a i
m n s r e t n u h e s k
```

monkeys
dogs
hunting
dragon
hamster
wild
capuchin
mouse
beasts
chickens
hunts
lambs
turtles
horse
snakes
rats
bear
pigeon
ostrich
hunters

Animal Puzzle 9

crocodiles
wildlife
pet
tree
grizzly
hedgehog
monkeys
dogs
hunting
dragon
hamster
wild
capuchin
mouse
beasts
chickens
lambs
turtles
horse
snakes

Animal Puzzle 10

l a i e g e c k o p e
g j u m p i n g s e c
o n n a m u p g p e h
s r i n m i a p i h a
t t e p o z k n g s s
r n i v e o s l e n e
i h b l a e b e o a s
c h l l c e k a n i t
h e a t a c b o b l a
d e s e r t m a o s r
c a m e l r a e b z e

rats
bear
pigeon
ostrich
gazelle
zookeeping
chipmunk
bobcat
koala
snail
beaver
gecko
desert
jumping
baboon
insects
chase
camel
sheep
puma

Made in the USA
San Bernardino, CA
19 December 2018